TIME MAKING THE FUTURE
A desperate effort of observing and utilizing time
Author: Joseph Bryan K

Copyright © 2013 Joseph Bryan K. All rights reserved.

Table of contents

Introduction		3
About the Author		4
Chapter 1	About time	5
Chapter 2	History	14
Chapter 3	Seasons	17
Chapter 4	Offspring line	21
Chapter 5	Development	24
Chapter 6	Patience	29
Chapter 7	Time is limited	33
Chapter 8	Changing your yesterday	38
Chapter 9	Speed of time	41
Chapter 10	Observing time	42
Chapter 11	Passing time	49
Chapter 12	God controlling time	53
Conclusion		56

INTRODUCTION

Welcome to the knowledge base of observing and utilizing time. Today, time is valued even more than visible and tangible valued things. Time is what determines all things in the future, it can create a bad or a good future according to the way a person utilize it. Time is present everywhere and waiting for people to use/utilize it. Utilize time day and night for a fast growing economic world. Anytime wasted will never come back again. Today, the question is not "who, where, or when should people observe time?" We should observe and utilize time all the 24 hours. Research have been made on time and other related things, and much emphasis is put on knowing what time is, but not knowing how to observe and utilize time. Time is running at a speed more than that of a will-o'-the-wisp, if you do not observe and utilize it – you will remain behind. In writing this novel, I aimed most, at showing how to observe and utilize time in order to change any thing that time may bring in future.

Furthermore, I welcome any suggestion or contributions that will contribute positively towards the knowledge of observing and utilizing time. This novel "Time making the future" fully meets its intended purpose and covers the gap that has always existed in matters concerning (observing and utilizing) time.

ABOUT THE AUTHOR

Joseph Bryan K

He is so much interested in Literature and Business. A person good at finding solutions for conditions that seems to be too difficult. Since 2001, he has got solutions for thousands of complicated situations brought about time. Today, he has much experience and knowledge of time. In this book, he has written about: [1] How to change your yesterday [2] Controlling what time is bringing in future [3] Living forever on earth in unlimited time. This book does not help a few people but all people in the world. The novel "Time making the future" was wrote for over 5 years. Read all chapters of this book, you will know how to get unlimited time on earth. This book is full of knowledge about time in every chapter.

CHAPTER ONE

ABOUT TIME

"Time is sold in exchange for money". We sell time to our employers to get money. Many people sit in their offices from morning to evening thinking that they are giving services only and these services are the reason as to why they are paid, but when in reality, they are giving away their time to their employers, bosses, and other peoples' businesses and they are paid for this time they spend on work. The time you spend seated in offices or else where working in other people's businesses, is not the only time for business but you should also have time for planning (to start) your own business, or putting in place a strong asset. No one wants to wakeup very early, leave workplace late, be abused or harassed by bosses; but because you want money you sell the time to your employers, bosses, and other people's business. Whereas this time you sell, you would have used it elsewhere in what is yours. People work everyday, almost 12 hours and above - this time they spend at work, they are selling it to their employers and bosses. For that matter, this is the reason why in developed countries people work hours; for example two, three, five or seven hours, and this shows that we are selling our days of life to our bosses, employers and other people's businesses. Whatever time or hour you take, it is deducted from your days of life; then if you spend your 12 hours at work, that means you have sold those 12 hours to your employers, bosses, or other people's businesses. In addition, at the end the employer or boss will pay your 12 hours you have spent on his/her business work in terms of money. Try to start your own business out side your job in order for you to spend your time in your own business tomorrow other than selling time to other people. If you start your business, you are going to sell time to yourself and you will retire when you are young. However, if you sell your time to your employers, bosses, and other people's businesses then you are going to sell your time to other people until your old age with out retiring. Its better you start a business of your own and start managing your time. Take a decision today and start a business at whatever price. Do not spend the all of your life on what is not yours, choose to make a business out side your job and give time to your own business. The job you have is not yours and any time you can leave that job. Now if today you leave that job and yet you have spent all your time on it whereas you did not take effort to start up some thing to spend some of your time on it, then all your time is wasted. However, if you started a business some years back then you have where to start. In addition, you are to spend your time in that business you started. The question is "if you stop working today, how long are you able to survive? Have you already setup a business or a great asset to move you all your life?" the time you spend elsewhere is not for any one else but for you your self therefore if you value time start using it on things which you will last with in future. Time shows signs and symbols. If you can see, watch, observe, and utilize time it will make for you tremendous wealth, but if you are blind about time, then time will make for you poverty. No one can start, add, or stop time except one that is GOD.

"Time is sold in exchange for an excuse". People have been put in prisons where they spend a lot of time for example days, weeks, months, or years and if they are businessmen then this makes their downfall, their businesses close up which leads them back to poverty. People pay their crimes in exchange with time. According to people, they know that prisoners pay for their crimes with the torture they find in prisons but in reality, they are paying with their time. And it's the reason as to why the judges do not give the kind of torture to be done to the one found guilty but give the amount of time a person will spend in prison for example days, weeks, months, year or years.

You should know much about time. Because we have time, we think, we breathe, we act, and we see, we hear, we eat, we talk, and we live. Time is everywhere, for as long as you are still living, you are living in the world of time. No one can prevent him/her self from time. Because time is the space we leave in, it is our environment. Without time, without you. Without time, without your birth. For a person to be born, it has to take a time of nine month when still in the belly. Without time, without where you are. Right now, you are adult because time drove you from childhood.

Without time without you, get rich. Time is what you are waiting for, to take you to your destiny. Moreover, if you are rich, then remember where you started from before getting rich. It has been along time. Therefore, if you are not rich now, then get to know that it is just a matter of time. In addition, remember that time is going to lead you to your destiny and become rich. Therefore time is what we are living in. many people have been found crying because they have wasted their time in terms of "work and not paid or half paid, divorced after a longtime in marriage, got best academic education but failed in life, and many other reasons. This is all about time. The decision is yours either you rule over time or you let the time rule over you.

Time to its self is equal and true but to many people it is not true and equal. Many people in the world have a different time count on their clocks, watches, phones, computers, and others. people themselves have let time not to be true to them and this is the reason has to why many people set their time in a different count for example some want their watch/clock to count some extra minutes like 5 or 10 from the time that is believed to be true. Whereas others want it to count less minutes than the original time. People have done this because of many reasons for example some want to do their work quickly, want to do some thing very fast, want to be early at events. This practice of forwarding some extra minutes like 5 or 10 from the original time looks like some one want to run faster than time. If you will go for a meeting at 12:00pm, and you forward your watch/clock some extra minutes like 10 or 20, this will make you be faster than time and you will be the first person at the meeting. In addition, you will be the earliest and there you will be the perfect one, whereas time is not true to you. We have to let time be true to us by making our selves to move with the original time. With this, we shall rule over time and it will not make us slaves.

      Time is like a will-o'-the-wisp that runs at a very quick speed and few people see it. Only few people can obverse time because it moves at a speed of light. Its time that makes young children to grow old, new products to become old, seeds to become trees and later cut for timber and timber for furniture. Time brings bad and good things. It is the way you observe and use time that makes it become soft or rough to you. Time have drove people to their old age when they are poor and with nothing, whereas it is time that had to bring them to their old age with a lot of wealthy, but because the way people know about time and the way they observe or use their time is different. Therefore, some people end up in wealth and others in poverty. People should know that every time we grow. Its better you start now to plan. People tend to see them selves the same every day. In addition, that is why they tend to imagine when others say to them statements like "you have grown, you have change, or you have height". Therefore, this is the time for you to start observing changes on you. If you want the truth about this yourself then take one month without facial care and without looking in the mirror and the next time, you look in it, you will know that everyday you have been growing and changing. If you do not walk with time, you are to stay as you are. Its time that drive poor people to become rich, villages to become cities, if you don't move with time then you will remain were you are, therefore get-up and walk with time.

People have tried to find means of observing time in order to rule over it and this is in the evolution of hourglass, clocks, watches, and other related means of time count devices. Clocks and watches have tried to make us know time and observe it to certain extend.

In this world, we had great leaders who thought of ruling forever but time made their downfall. They did not look at the future but they just ruled according to how they wanted. I appreciate the countries and their leaders who have taken effort to observe and utilize time well. They have decided to do good in order to save the good reputation of their countries, their leadership, and themselves. You should take an example from the United States of America government and the presidents how they lead. The presidents of America accept whatever comes from the votes during elections. They do not come into leadership by force and they do not remain on leadership if they are won by elections. They keep their dignity and respect while even looking in the future in order not to leave bad history. This means that they are observing and utilizing time as well as moving with time. Time will always move with this kind of governance. Some leaders in the world do not look at what time will bring but they just use their powers the way they want and then time leads to their downfall. Look in history all those who where great leaders who misused their power knowing that they will rule forever are no long present. Its time that drove years and they disappeared but leaving bad history. Therefore, if we become great we should do good things to the people because time is coming when you will be in history of those who did well or bad. Therefore, mind a bout your offspring and start to do good. Never allow time to show you what is of today but it should show you even the future. Because by a blink of an eye you who is still young you are going to become old and you who is ruling today, next time will be another person ruling who will want to reward you for good leadership or take vengeance on you for your bad leadership.

Money and time are close friends; if you have a lot of one of them then you have a lot of the other. Moreover, if you have a little of one of them then you have a little of the other. That is why it is said, "Time is money" and "money is time". If you have money, you will work for only 2 to 5 hours at your businesses/office and have other hours elsewhere exploring new things. Nevertheless, if you do not have money you will work for 12 to 24 hours. Therefore, those with money have a lot of time than those without. Money buys time and time buys money. The only difference between them is that money buys time - easy and whenever it wants whereas time buys money through difficulty and at a specified moment. For an employer to get workers it is very easy because everyone is looking for a job but for a jobseeker to get a job, it can take months or years. The employers want you to use your time in their businesses while the job seekers want to sell their time to the employers' businesses. People should know that they are not only giving labor to their employers but also they are giving out their time to their employers. Start a business today at whatever cost and manage it with time then time will drive it into a billion dollars earning business. Make many assets then you will get money and time, and for this reason you are likely to retire at any age. If you have a lot of money then you are likely to have a lot of time. You can also use this time to make productive activities especially that come out of your talent as games and sports for example Golf, and this bring for you tremendous wealth.

No one can separate money and time because wherever there is money there is time also. "Every money got, there has to be time spent" even if money has been given to you as a gift, the one who has given it to you has spent time first to get it. Towns and cities are crowded because of time and money. People move out of homes to spend time in towns and cities looking for money. When there is getting money there is also spending of time. The researchers and novelists, take a lot of time researching and writing then at the end, they get a lot of money. Use your time to buy money then after getting money buy time and this bought time will make for you more money. Work for money first and later make money work for you. If you are working for others then start a business out side your job and in future people will work for you. Employers work few hours for example two, three or five hours but the employees work according to the working time. Today the choice is yours either you start a business out side your job that you may also one time become a business owner with a lot of time, or remain an employee forever with little time only for resting.

Although money and time are together, there are stages of getting each of them. Time is first and money is second then time and money both become third. You first give in your time then money will come to you. Use that money to buy time. If you give in your time today at an earlier age and start now, you will get money and later on in the future you will have both time and money. Start now to invest. Start your own business and in the future, you will retire at an earlier age and have both time and money. If you do not use your time at a young age then expect to struggle in your old age. Time is capable of being the worst enemy of man but also capable of being the best friend of man. Time does not look behind it looks in front. It moves in a straight path and runs at a speed more than that of a will-o'-the-wisp or a blink of an eye. Time keeps on pulling all of us at its speed and it is successful with this every microsecond. This is the reason as to why no one can refuse to grow but every one find himself when he/she was a young child but now he/she is an old person. There are many reasons and views as to why people are born very young and later come up to grow very old but we don't know which of them is to be followed if we are to a small extend able to find solution of controlling this quick growth. Is it the environment?

Is it the air breathed? Is it what we see? Is it in our bodies? Is it in our minds? Let us observe one of the above, let us take an example of our minds. We are the one to decide to either use our minds or not. The mind is strong; everything in our life base on the mind. Whatever good thing you get is not for the whole you but for your mind. Moreover, the punishment a person gets is not to the whole body but to the mind. The mind is responsible for feeling, tasting, smelling, seeing, and hearing. If the mind is responsible for these five senses, which act with in the body, then it is even responsible for changes of the body. Your growth from childhood to adulthood to some extend the responsible may be for your mind. Because nothing happens to the body and the minds does not get to know.

   You should not allow the speed of time to interfere too much with your growth. It is the mind than controls the interference of the speed of time to your growth. You can walk and move with time but never allow time to drive you on its speed the way it wants. If you leave your mind to be driven by time then time will pull your all body and you who was young you will find your self - old very quickly. However, if your mind is stable then time will remain moving with you but it will not interfere or pull you too much in your growth. The mind that does not store information and that does not do things repeatedly its body is likely to grow at a very speed rate. Take an example of teachers, lecturers, professors, and others. These people take long to grow in their bodies because their minds are ever repeating the same topics, lessons, books, and novels every year moreover to different classes every day. This kind of repeating things by reading, teaching, or doing the same things; makes it difficult for time to pull you easily because time moves in the straight path and at a very quick speed. Then if your mind is ever repeating things repeatedly, you will walk and move with time but time will not pull your growth. Today take your time and start reading bookings. Get your Bible, novels, textbooks, and magazines then read repeatedly. Time will not pull a mind that have a rotating movement that circulates in one place repeatedly. This makes time to run on its own for a failure to pull what does not move straight, that only rotates. If your mind does not repeat things daily then time will pull it and drive it so fast. Teach yourself to read books every day. I have brought this example to show you how people who 'do something over and over again' take long to show growth on their bodies and remain to count years but they do not resemble these years. Most of the people who do things over and over again for example the teachers, lecturers, professors, footballers, singers, soldiers, and others they experience a slow growth but this slow growth happens to them when they are still in their fields. Once some one stops doing what he/she has been doing, then the growth will start immediately.

It is GOD who control over the time and the seasons, the sun and the moon, the day and the night. this is revealed in Bible in the book of Genesis 1:3 to 5, Genesis 6:3, Exodus 20:12, Joshua 10:12 to 14, Isaiah 38:2 to 5, and many others.

Where there is time there is everything. All crowded and busy cities in the world show presence of time. Because people have time, they move from one place to another looking for money.

CHAPTER TWO

HISTORY

The Historians believe that "History repeats it's self" this means what is "past will come back again or something will come looking the same as that of the past". This is not the same with time "time will never repeat its self" and it will never come back. If you have a history of 01/Jan/2001 that at welcoming new year there was great fire works all over the cities, this history will repeat it's self in 01/Jan/2002, 2003, 2004, or 2013 but the time will not repeat its self that's why you keep on celebrating 1st Jan welcoming new year at different years. For if, you celebrated 01/Jan/ 2011 as New Year when you are 25 years then the next time you will celebrate 01/Jan/2012 when you are 26 years. Therefore, we have to move with time such that we do not regret the past. People who move with time they have given in their best to use their time now that they gain it in future.

People have been asking themselves questions for example, "if time was reversed, it would have been reversed" or "if time was forwarded it would have been forwarded". These questions appear in people's minds when they get troubles, misfortune, problems, discouragement, and many others. These questions like "if time was reversed," mean that this person would have done something to stop the current situation to occur. The truth is that time once past cannot come back; it is the history that comes back repeatedly. Therefore, you have to be observant of the time that the history does not come back. We can hinder the history to repeat its self but time moves in a straight path and does not rotate as history does. You can know what history is bringing again but for time is new every period so you cannot know what it brings and you can only control it from bring unwanted events or things if you are very observant. History happens in unspecified time therefore we have to know how to handle time that we can hinder and obstruct history to repeat its self or taking place again. Today many people have sayings like "if time was reversed" this is what many people have in their thoughts. Many things of the sort been seen through music, dramas, plays, and films/movies like "Time machine" and "Out of time". Today people pass through bad situations caused by time but they always wish if time can reverse then it would have reverse. This is because some people have wasted a lot of time and wants to gain it, yet others have problems and they are sure that if time can reverse they can change what cause these problems to occur such that they do not occur again. For example if it was an accident of a vehicle where one was severely injured, he/she will have a thought "if time can reverse, at that day I would not move that way or I would have stayed at home. Time has made many to be in regrets.

Time is what puts in place and what removes. It has brought civilization, development; and removes primitive living. Time has brought cities, towns; and removes forests, bushes, and wild animals. It has changed seed into plants and trees. Time brings people and takes them away in terms of birth and death .Time has made people one family, and it has scattered and separated them. It has caused cries and it has brought happiness. If in January, a person is crying because of poverty then time will drive him/her to another month (June, October, or December) where he/she will get rich and be happy. It is time that drives you to a new day full of happiness and joy. Time is a straight path runner and drives every person the way it wants except when knowledge of time is with such a person. It calls what no one can think of and it sends what we do not expect. If one is leaving the earth then he/she is leaving time. Those who are born are entering time and those who die are leaving time but time remains. If there is no time, no growth will take place therefore the earth is like how it is because of time. On the earth, it is where the time lives. If time is not on the earth, the earth cannot stand-alone. Time cannot separate from the earth. This means that if we are living, we cannot separate from time.

CHAPTER THREE

SEASONS

In winter season, work becomes very difficult. Most of the people work in summer season and almost have or remain with little work to do during winter. This make the days in winter seasons to pass away unutilized well. Many people stay at home because moving to work is difficult in winter. Some of people work in open places, outside buildings for example the builders, farmers, drivers, and others. Therefore, winter season limits a big number of people from work.

In Hawaii the fiftieth state of United States of America summer days are longer than winter days which makes the people of Hawaii to have enough period of time to involve in fishing, farming, industrial work, and developing the State. Hawaii's sugar and pineapple industries have developed because sugar canes and pineapple are the important and major cash crops grown in United State. These have made the people of Hawaii to carry on farming, fishing, and industrial work due to the longer summer days/season than winter.

Take this example from the old legend of the Hawaiian people. "Once upon a time, a boy in Hawaii named Ma-ui was angry with the fast movement of the sun and how short was the movement of the days in winter seasons. He thought about what he could do, but he did not come up with a solution. Later he asked his grand mother what he could do about the situation. The grandmother told Ma-ui to have with him 16 strongest ropes and make a trap in the way of the sun. Therefore, he hid somewhere and watched as the first leg of the sun was moving to the mountain where he had set out the ropes. Then the first leg of the sun was catch in one of the ropes and the other leg was catch. This resulted into a big fight between the sun and Ma-ui. At this time, the sun increased its heat to make Ma-ui lose, but he insisted and fought the sun using a magic stone ax. Then after along time in the war, the sun gave up and surrendered, so the sun accepted to do whatever Ma-ui would want it to do. Ma-ui said to the sun, "you must not move fast across the sky". Then the sun accepted and promised Ma-ui that it will move very slowly in the 6 months of the year, so the days were longer. In addition, in the other 6 months of the year the sun would move very first. After these agreements, Ma-ui let the sun to move on with its journey. These agreements made the days to bee longer and people had enough time for fishing, farming, industrial work, and other activities.

Everything has its advantage and disadvantage. Daylight serving time (DST) has helped some people but again it is not true to time. In observing and utilizing time we do not need to rewind or forward the clock but on the other hand, it has helped in energy serving and having more daylight hours for business, sports and other activities that need a longer day especially in USA. In Hawaii, the clock is advance to make sunrise time close to 7:00 am and in Alaska some people have used Daylight serving time (DST) but again there has been a statewide move to abolish it. Observing and utilizing time is different basing on the climatic conditions of an area. Some areas experience summer, winter, autumn, and spring which is not the case in other regions. In Alaska's tundra region, observing and utilizing time is very different from other areas. During winter in Alaska's tundra region(s) there is almost no sunlight whereas during summer months it receives sunlight almost all the time. From the end of March to the end of September, the sun does not set at all. Moreover, from September to March the sun does not rise. Here night lasts for six months and day last for six month. The way people use their time in this region is very different from other regions. Much of the Work and activities take place almost during the six months from the end of March to the end of September because of the presence of daylight. In addition, work is difficult in other six months of the year. Utilizing time in activities is very low; therefore, people do other things.

       Time makes new products to expire and become old. Try to buy and use a product today because everyday it spends in the freezer or supermarket or shop it is moving to its expiry date. Some people do not focus too much on the manufacturing date and the expiry date of the product. If the manufacturing date of a product is 01/Jan/2013 and has an expiry date of 31/Dec/2013, then its benefit to a person in January to November is not the same as that of December. Everyday a product is moving to its expiry date, let take an example of the lakeshore, if you are in water that reaches your head when you stand at the bottom of the lake and you start moving towards the shore, the water level goes on slowing down and at walking your body will go on rising from water. In addition, the water level that was up on your head will now be down at your feet. Same on products, from the manufacturing date the product goes on losing benefits until the expiry date. Learn how to do things very fast. There is no time to waste in postponing things to do. Always the first information is valued than the second information, therefore if you are to get some thing always get it fast. Latecomers always eat bones. Start doing some things now when it is still early before they become impossible. You have time now - then start now. Never wait for tomorrow. The tomorrow will become un-ending story/day because everyday you will say, "I will do tomorrow". People have wasted much time in postponing work (to) tomorrow. Their tomorrow does not end. In addition, many people become aged (old) when they have not done what they wanted to do. Time is not there to use it in everything you like (according to your emotions). Use time in productive activities, which will make you successful in future. Some people forward their O'clock one hour such that they get one hour added on their sleeping time. What reason can a person give in forwarding his/her clock? Is it a reason to increase your working hours? If so, then Daylight serving time (DST) will be important but again in your job you work only the hours you signed for example 2 hours at work. May be you add this one time in your own business. All these changes made on time can be helpful but time remains moving as usual. It does not forward any minute, it continue moving forward on its original time and count. However, in all conditions never allow time to live you behind because if time leaves you, you will never find it again. It is already wasted. Time waits for no man.

Our clocks and watches when counting time ends at 12 hours and others 24 hours then they go back to 1 hour but for time, it moves forward and does not have an end of count. From AB, it may be 17633880 hours past. Nevertheless, because our counting ends at 12 hours and 24 hours we only go on counting years for example 2013 years have past from AB.

CHAPTER FOUR

OFFSPRING LINE

People take long time when sleeping and resting. Let say that 90% of the people sleep during night and 10% sleep at day, while of these 10% only 8%work at night and rest during day, 2% work night and day and they don't have specific time of resting/sleeping but they rest at any hour when they are completely tired and can't go on without working. Why does the big number of people the 90% sleep at night? The 15% sleep a little and wakeup for some purposes like prayers, business planning, and other activities. The 75% sleep all night long. This is an old way of living your life following the offspring even today in this working world. This was the way of living of the people of long ago in the past.

The reason why people sleep a lot at night comes right from their ancestors of long ago and because the people today are their seeds, they have those characters, activities, behaviors, and way of living that keep on following their lines. Long ago, people worked day and sleep at late evening/night because there where nothing like enough light besides the light of the stars and the moon. This limited their activities and work because they feared attacks from wild animals that often moved at night. Wild animals attacked and killed many people and others wounded. So walking and working at night was not easy therefore, it did not take place at night. This made people of long ago to work during day and sleep from late evening to early morning. Before man discovered fire, the only light at night was that of the stars and moon, so when man was inside his small hut, and cave, he could see no light and the results was sleeping until morning. The darkness inside the hut/cave during night could not make man to do any activity or work because there was no light at all.

      Take an example in the current world today when electricity light goes off at late evening (7:00pm to), a big number of people sleep earlier than usually. But when the electricity is on at night a big number of people sleep at 12:00am midnight due to presence of light, watching TV, films, music, planning business, studies, work, shops open, and many others. The discovery of fire by man led to a very great change on the people of long ago. They used fire to light - out and inside their homes. This paved a way to increase the time of working and making activities instead of sleeping in the late evening. Man lighted fire as light at night and used that time to compose poems, tell stories, do simple activities, and many others. In addition, from that moment man increased hours at night of doing other things before sleeping. Now today we are not only having fire as light but also electricity light. However, this has not changed people from sleeping early or having long hours of rest or sleeping. Absence of light before and after the evolution of fire by man made the people of long ago to sleep very early. This way of living is following the offspring and the lines of the people of long ago until/even now. If you do not change then change will change you but not as much as you would have changed your self. And this is why today a big number of people have increased on the hours of going to sleep from the hours of people of long ago they used to sleep. This has come from the change changing them. If today people accept to change themselves, they will have few hours in resting or sleeping. Sleeping too much is wastage of time. It is health to sleep little or few hours. In addition, businesspersons take little and few hours in sleeping. Every one would expect them to have excessive resting because they have a lot of money but they wake up in late night and plan for their businesses, look for ideals, and make strategies. This has made them to utilize their time well and come up with success and prosperity in their businesses. They do not have time to waste in excessive rest or sleeping. Try to change your self, wakeup early to pray and plan for your business/future. Remember wasted time will never come back. Never allow a day or night to pass unutilized.

CHAPTER FIVE

DEVELOPMENT

Civilization and development have led to the establishment of towns, cities, and modern places where people have made settlement and experienced high standards of living. The development, which includes setup of towns, cities, and modern places, have decreased the number of wild animal that earlier attacked people of long ago and they did not work or do any outside activity during night. Among the inevitable night activities was fishing which took place during night. The anglers went late evening and come back early morning whereas others built near lakeshores. Today, these wild animals are no longer there to make work difficult at night, but still a small number of people work during night. In addition, this does not mean that all people should start to work at night but this brings in all people to join and open businesses day and night, in order not to let the night to come and pass when there is no work - taking place. Today we no longer have wild animals to hinder us from working or opening our businesses (even) at night. Other excuses people give of not opening businesses at night include theft and robbery. This is very easy to stop it happening at night. If all the people come together and start working day and night opening their businesses, also the customers will be available day and night, they will be many in towns and cities, which will make security to be in place. Therefore, these thieves and robbers will fear the crowd as it is during day.

Time is running at high speed therefore utilize day and night well and useful. For a quick and speed development in an area, working should take place day and night. Take an example of the buildings or flats in the cities and towns how they are built very first, its because the builders and workers built day and night and this have led to the faster development of the cities. In addition, if people want to get prosperity very quickly they should work day and night. Take an example of hotels, restaurants, and supermarkets how they work day and night. They open 24 hours and they have workers for day and for night. To a certain extend, this has reduced unemployment and bringing wealth to the business owners. Therefore, to bring employment, wealth, and development we have to open all businesses even at night to fill or use the time wasted at night. Start now and plan working at night as the factories, industries, and hotels do, then you will have doubled the money or income you get in the day. In the 12 hours of night you waste, you lose millions of dollars. All people should look at this strategy and try to use these 12 hours of the night. This does not mean you do not sleep or rest at night - the directors, managers and bosses of industries, restaurants, supermarkets, hotels, petrol stations and factories that work day and night get enough rest and sleeping time but they employ other people who usually work at night. They employ trustworthy people to run their businesses at night. They let other people make money for them in the 12 hours of the night.

   Observe and utilize the day and the night. Do not allow any time to pass because you will not bring it back. If you want to bring time back, you have also to waste time again - in trying to find the wasted time back. It will be better to utilize time that is in front of you and not look behind for what you have not got or done in the past time. Imagine if it were day only in 24hours, people would have no specified time to rest or sleep. Some would have even worked 24hours and get little rest or sleeping time in other hours of the next day. This would have brought development at a faster state. Today we have electricity light during night that enables people to do work and activities during night like companies, industries, petrol stations, hotel, restaurant, and other businesses that work day and night because at night there is light of electricity bulbs. In addition, other events like sports for example football, which took place during day, only is now taking place even at night. Therefore, if 16 matches are to take place in 16 days now due to the emphasis of working day and night, the matches will take 8 days where by one is played day and another one night hence saving time and utilizing it. Moreover, this has been possible due to electricity light, but imagine if there was no night and it is only day 24 hours.

Time is money and money is time. Any time you waste, you lose money. If you use your time to get money, you will get it. If you use daytime to get money in your work/business then what about nighttime - the 12hours you relax with out doing any business or work. In these 12 hours of the night, you are missing and losing millions Dollars. The time you put in for your business is the amount of money you get. if your business (for example hotel) work only day then that's the little money you will get but if it works day and night then that is the much more amount you will get. Anytime you waste will not come back, likewise the money you lose in that wasted time will not come back to you but gone forever, and if it was in circulation then it did not pass/come your way. In wasted time, it is where people waste their opportunities of being at the top and being billionaires.

If some cities need 100years to develop and look like New York city then people will need to work day and night to divide a 100 years by 2 to be 50 years so as to make it faster. These are all ways of saving time while utilizing it. If people work day only it takes 100years but if they work day and night that will be 50 years for day and 50 years for night. If you have a business, and you are to retire at 60 years according to your business income, profits, and the growth of your asset columns; now if you make your business to work even at night, you will retire at 30 years. Because you are working day and night, so this divides the 60 into 2 to be 30 years. Also if you where to retire at 50, now if your business operate day and night, you will retire at 25. This brings double profit that also doubles the money you invest in other assets hence diving the retiring age by two. The speed of the growth and development of your business is determined on the hours your business opens. If you open your business at 10:00am your daily income is not as that of a person who open very early in the morning. You may give many excuses but you are losing a lot of money. Likewise, the business that works day only is not the same as that which work day and night. For example, hotels, restaurants, and others that some workday only, others work night only, and others work day and night. the three businesses earn different daily income where by the one which work day only makes much money that which work night only and the other which work day and night is much earning that the other two businesses.

      The more time you make your business to be in service is the more your daily income will be. If your business operate day only and you are to get rich in 10 years, now if you make your business work day and night you are to get rich in 5 years. Likewise, if your business operates day only and you have 4 years to get rich, now if you work day and night, it will be 2 years for you to get rich and your business to grow. Take an example in building a flat where building takes place only day is different from that which its building takes place day and night. For the flat its building process take place only day, in two months will be at first floor while that whose building take place day and night in one month will be at second floor. Business is also like that, if you and your neighbors sell the same products, and make services only day. Both of you will not have much differences in your daily income, but if you happen to open services even during night then you will have doubled the income from that of your neighbors and that which you have been getting while still carrying out services during day only.

In these businesses which do services day and night is where the richest people especially the investors have invested their money. For example petrol stations, industries, factories, supermarkets, transport network, communication networks and others. These businesses work day and night, which leaves no gap for resting and dormancy in their businesses. The reason as to why criminals use the night to break up people's shops and business places to steal is because these businesses don't work at night which gives the thieves and robbers a free environment with out people hence stealing and robbing business products and goods in people's shops and business places. This leads these growing businesses to go back to zero and their owners turn back into financial struggles. If robbers and thieves steal business products and goods then the owner is off truck in going at the top. If this fear of robbers and thieves is the reason of not opening businesses at night, then what about businesses like hotels, restaurants, petrol stations, industries, factories and others which work even at night. If that was a strong reason then these businesses will not be working at night. However, these businesses use a very little a mount of money (from big profits they get in the night) and put it in security companies to secure the business area. Start planning this today your businesses will grow very fast.

CHAPTER SIX

PATIENCE

There is no day that begins at midnight that will not come to morning and from morning to evening and from evening to midnight again. In addition, any day at morning will likewise come to night and night to day. Without fail, morning will come to noon and noon to evening then to night and night to day-morning. If you are waiting for something don't say "it has delayed" or "I have waited for so long and am tired", and then this makes you tire out of what you are waiting for. If a person says " Next week" be sure that by all mean next week will come to pass and your will start to call its days "Today, tomorrow, or yesterday ". May-be someone promised you something next week or next month or next year. The next week, next month, next year will happen and you will start to call the days in it "yesterday, today, or tomorrow". For example, examinations, parties, business deals, meetings, outings or anything you want to prepare for or be ready for, for the next week, month, year, or years, these next week, month, year, or years will happen and you will call its days "yesterday, today, or tomorrow". Therefore, do not sit and relax thinking that this next day, next week, next month, or next year is very far. You have to know that is very near at hand. If you are preparing something in future for yourself, wife, children, family, parents, relatives, friends, business, state, country, or the world let say in the coming year or years to come, do not sit and relax or wait thinking that these years are very far and then you will do or prepare what you want to do any time. Just start now and prepare for it. Be fast at doing things - the earlier the better. For these years to come in future, be it one, two, three, five, or seven years, will happen and you will call the days in them "yesterday, today, or tomorrow. For example, if you are preparing for an event on 04/May/2051 then it will happen and you will say, "I have prepared today for many years back".

People when they do not have they instead promise. They promise in days, weeks, months, a year or years forgetting that these "days, weeks, months, or years will come to pass and they will call the days in them "yesterday, today, tomorrow". people would have promised what they are sure of but not what they're not sure of, because by all means time will come to that specific day a person made a promise yet he/she don't have what he/she promised to give out. Promise is a debt; if a person owes you then you are in debt to somebody. When a person is borrowing something for example money, he or she say "I will return it or pay it next week, month, year or years, not knowing where he or she will get the money to pay what he or she is borrowing. But because he or she see a week, month, year or years as they are very far and before they come or reach he or she will have paid the debt. People should know that time and days are running very fast.

According to astronomy/astrophysics, 'the earth is moving at a very high speed in space'; but according to the nature of man, people see along period from morning to evening. In addition, that is why some people during the morning say, "I wonder when the evening will come or reach and I go this or that way, go to a cinema, outing, coffee at the café, or go back home". These people forget that by a blink of an eye, the morning will come to noon and noon to evening then everyone will do what he/she wanted to do or go where he/she wanted to go. Take an example of a farmer who keeps cattle, grow crops and plants that take months or years to be ready for harvesting and serve as food, raw materials, products, and others. The farmers already know the years these plantations take from planting to harvesting but they understand that these years will happen and turn into days and become "yesterday, today, or tomorrow" and they will start to harvest. In planting these plantations, they do not care how many years it will take for their growth even if they take five years or above. The weeks, months, a year or years that you are waiting for, will one time come to be days and start to call them "yesterday, today, or tomorrow".

        We have to be patience in whatever we do. If we are not patient then we are likely to waste a lot of time. There is no morning that will not come to noon and noon - that will not come to evening, then to midnight, and to morning a gain. We have to be patient in all we do. We should not have a desire that time should run very fast because we have appointments or meetings in the hours to come. Do not decide to make some thing to obstruct your following of time for example going to entertainment in order that you do not notice (the movement of) time. Patience in time is need. Instead of moving to entertainment/fun for a reason of running time (obstructing your mind that you do not notice the movement of time), use that time to make useful things. Time is precious; if you have time, you have hope of reaching your destiny. Do not look at yourself as failure when you are still living. Whichever age you may have, you can make it; success is not limited to age. Even if you are very old in age, you still need to struggle for success because this success will not only end at you but it will even go to your offspring. Many young researchers tried out research on certain things for a thousand times and later came up with solution when they are old people but today their offspring are enjoying what they (their grand parents) introduced. Keep on using your time everyday then you will come up with some thing that will help the world and this will bring tremendous wealth to you and your offspring. In a thousand times you try out a research on something, there is only one time that will lead you to your destiny of what you are researching. People's signatures don't resemble and are very difficult to forge but if a person keeps on trying a certain signature to make it exact as (the original) that of the owner, then in a 1000 times he/she tries it out, there is one time it will look exactly the same. Time will not stop adding on our age, and will not stop making people older every day. However, in time its where (our success is) we have to make our success and enjoy good living in every time added on our age such that when we grow old we don't regret our being unhappy in all of our (youth age) life.

CHAPTER SEVEN

TIME IS LIMITED

Time is the strong reason why morning will move to evening and evening to night and night to morning again. With the movement of time the days, weeks, months, and years will without fail come to pass. Therefore, do not waste any time because time wasted will never come back. Now start doing something today because what you plan or prepare to do next days, week, month ,year or years is to be done today and now but not a day ,a week, a month, or a year later.

Some people have a say "Time is the worst enemy of man". Whereas others say, "devil or Satan is the worst enemy of man" but the truth is that "the devil or Satan is the first worst enemy of man and followed by time which is the second worst enemy of man". Moreover, the devil or Satan has his enemy that is "Time". This is revealed in Bible in the book of Revelation 12:12 ………………………."woe for the earth and for the sea, because the Devil has come down to you having great anger, knowing he has a short period of time"…………………………………….

In a day, the morning that comes to evening and evening to night and night to morning again, that day is already gone. Time cannot come back even a single microsecond that is why the clock when counting or showing time moves clockwise or forward. No normal clock/watch can count anti-clockwise/backward. All clocks count clockwise or forward. This is the reason why morning will come to noon and noon to evening and evening to midnight and night to morning again.

Because time is running quickly and days move at a faster speed, you should take little but enough time in resting and sleeping. You should not take excessive resting because if you take excessive resting or sleeping at night you are wasting a lot the time. Also at night, people pass time in entertainment, games, and other things. This will close the space for thinking, planning for the future, and others. By being busy in other work and activities during day does not give gap to think and plan therefore instead of entertainment and funs after work spare some time of planning the future. Most of the people after working they (enjoy free moments) spend time in leisure, luxury, entertainment, movies but you have to know that you cannot bring back the time you spend or pass.

If you cannot move with time then it will leave you behind. Many people waste a lot of time due to failure of moving with time. Many old people have many regrets about their failure in life. This is all about time. Once you stop somewhere, time will not wait for you. You will get to know that you had to do something great when you are old and have no much time (and ability). Some of the people when they suffer in life they mostly blame their parents of not preparing for their future. Do not be a parent(s) who his/her child/children will blame of not taking care to prepare his/her/their future. It is the high time to start preparing for yourself and your family's future. Now is the time to work for a good future. Never allow any time to pass unutilized. The more you observe/use any time you get /have, the more you subtract on the (your) retirement age from work. Time will never wait for any man or woman. Once you move from the straight path of time, time will leave you behind. Time has no friend and has no mercy that it will be kind and wait for anyone. If you call time, it will not turn and look at you. It moves looking forward only. It will not make any deal with anyone, it behaves as if it is deaf yet it hears. If time leaves you behind, it will not listen to your excuses. Time can listen to people who have given in their best to move with it. Today the choice is yours either to fail or to be successful, either to waste time or to utilize time. You will never find people who utilize time anywhere begging time to wait for them. Past is past will never come back. In this pasted and wasted time, it is where people lose their opportunities. Opportunities move to almost all directions heading to every one, but when the opportunities reach at you when you are not active, it will just pass and go elsewhere for a reason (being) that you did not welcome it, it did not receive the hospitality; at the time it reached at you, you were not active. Opportunities do not enter where there is wasting of time but they only enter where there is observing and utilizing of time. If you are wasting time now, the opportunities are going to pass over to another person who is active now. Time wait for no man. Now is the time for you to start moving with time and then all opportunities will move in your direction. Time wasted will never come back. In addition, opportunities wasted will never come back. Time will never wait for you. If it brings an opportunity in your way and you do not receive it, time will drive it into another direction of someone else. You should be watchful such that you do not waste time and opportunities. You have all abilities to move with time therefore never allow time to leave you. No one should deceive him/her self with false reasons that time will wait for him/her. Time does not look back therefore if you are to move with time you should not look back also. Do not rejoice for yesterday's great deeds because yesterday is already past but make rejoice of the great deeds you have done today while also preparing what you will do tomorrow to make it a day of great deeds. Time will not wait for you when you focus on the past, it will just move on, and at the time you will turn back from focusing at the past, there will be no where to find time.

  Time is in everyplace, everywhere you go you find time. Today most of the people value time so much. Time should be valued even more than money. Money can buy time and time can buy money. The difference is that money buys time in terms of labor but time buys money in all ways. If you value time, you are valuing your self. Time will value a person only if that person also value time - by moving with it. Time has no friend but can be a friend to only those people who observe and utilize it urgently. Moreover, those people who get rewards and good things from time are those who observe and utilize it. Time rewards wealthy, success and destiny to those who move with it. If you move with time then wait for your success any time. If a person values time then time will be honest to him/her. Time pass through many things, it pass through wealth, success, destiny, happiness, peace, freedom, and other things but only those who move with time can get these things. For those who do not move with time they will not pass that way. It is only time that pass that way. If you do not move with time then time will not take you that way. Today decide to move with time, you will benefit and gain from it. Time wasted is worthy millions of dollars therefore never waste any time.

Today decide to move with time then you will be able to control whatever time is bringing. Whoever wants his/her future to be the way he/she wants it to be, he/she has to move with time. People have success because they decided to move with time. Time is what turns seeds into trees, babies into old people, therefore if you move with time it will turn your small business in a very large company in future. In addition, it will even turn your ideas into reality. So move everything with time, then you will be prosperous in future. You should not bring any reason of not observing and utilizing time. You have to leave all reasons aside and observe time. To a certain extent, the time you observe and utilize sometimes fill/cover the reasons you have of not utilizing time. No excuse you can give of not observing and utilizing time. The time you waste in excuses will never come back again. In addition, the opportunities you lose in wasted time would have been part of your way to success. Remember time is money and money is time. Both money and time, each can buy the other. Therefore, in wasting time you also waste millions of dollars. Moreover, it will cost you millions of dollars to buy that (wasted) time or (if possible even) opportunities.

Never worry about tomorrow, tomorrow is another day therefore look at today and now. If you insist on worrying about tomorrow you will continue worrying forever, worrying about some thing does not remove or change it. What you do is what changes or removes anything. Start today to do some thing to make your tomorrow a better day. Time is limited. If you keep on worrying, you will continue wasting time. If you move with time, you will control whatever it brings. Time waits for no man; it goes with those who go and moves with those who move. Time has been present since the creation of the earth and until now, it is still moving. It has seen many generations right from the beginning until now. Time will not wait for any one. It will not sympathize with any person. You are not the first one to live in the world of time, many people have moved with time and become prosperous in life therefore keep on moving with time and you will get success in life.

CHAPTER EIGHT

CHANGING YESTERDAY

You cannot change your yesterday because past is past will never come back but you can change the yesterday of tomorrow. Today is the yesterday of tomorrow. You have to start today and be active everyday. You can change your today and your tomorrow by today. If you use the time, you have today then your today will become a 'meaningful day' tomorrow. You can change your tomorrow by today because today is the yesterday of tomorrow. The only way to change your yesterday is to become active today because today is the yesterday of tomorrow and the future. Moreover, if you do this on daily basis you will never regret your yesterday. You are regretting about yesterday because you were not active and did not used it well. If you look back then you waste the time you put in looking at the past. In addition, if you insist on looking at the past, then you are going to waste the time forever. We should use the time we have now to make our tomorrow's yesterday a day to be glad in. yesterday will never end. You will continue to have yesterdays forever but to change these yesterdays you have to be active today and now. Because today is the yesterday of your tomorrow and this will continue forever. Every day that comes is new therefore whatever you do - do not focus on the yesterday's great deeds you done but focus on the deeds of today such that they also become great like those of yesterday. Keep on doing like this you will be called the great. There is no time to waste in what has past. If yesterday, you were not active then start today to be active. In addition, if you made yesterday great then what about today, even today should be great and all days to come.

Today is precious, if you do not use it, it is already gone and will never come back but if you use it well then you will gain much from it. If you are glad and rejoicing today in the great activities you deed yesterday, you should stop now and look at today what you should do to make even today great like yesterday because today will become the yesterday of tomorrow therefore if you don't do great today what will you be glad in tomorrow. Ask yourself what have you done today that will make you be glad-in tomorrow. Therefore, let everyday be of doing something productive.

You can only change your past by doing great today because today is the past of tomorrow and the future. The only way of changing the past is by utilizing well your today. You can only change your past by doing great today because today is the past of tomorrow (and the future). The only way of changing the past is by utilizing and doing great activities today such that (every) tomorrow you will say, "Yesterday past and it will never come back but I managed to utilize it and use it well. The only way to change your yesterday is by doing great activities today because today is the yesterday of tomorrow. Yesterday, today, and tomorrow will never end. All days in front/ahead of today are yesterday, today, and tomorrow. Everyday in future will come to pass/take place and be yesterday, today, or tomorrow. Therefore, we should not look at the past; leave alone the past, the past is only in history. Moreover, even if history repeats its self, the event that will repeat in future will not be the exact one that happened in the past but it will just resemble the same as that which happened in the past. Nothing of the past will come back exactly the same (original). You should not look back at your background as an obstacle for your success. Success is what you make. The more you are active in all days is the more you become close to your success. In addition, you will never regret your yesterday as a wasted day. If you utilize all days, there will be no yesterday as a wasted day. If you are to change your yesterday then today is the day that will change your yesterday. If you use your today well you will never regret about your yesterday or past. Yesterday came as today has come but you were not active therefore be active today such that when tomorrow come, you would already changed your yesterday of your tomorrow.

CHAPTER NINE

SPEED OF TIME

When a child is born, by a blink of an eye, he or she is old and this person will start to say, "I have been very young in the past 20 or 30 years but look now I have grown old". "I used to wakeup early for school, but now I wakeup early for work", "I used to spare time for reading books but now I spare time for planning my businesses and work.", "we used to play football, basketball but now I have grown old enough my body is no longer able". Meditate how you were when you were young what you used to do. Imitate on the time from your childhood to your adulthood whether it's a small period or a long period……After thinking about that period……now have you seen how days, weeks, months, and years run faster at a quick state. It is very difficult for one to observe the way he or she grows; we grow every hour and every day. Some people find themselves fat, tall, and grown old when they do not know. Some people have been told how they have grown big or so faster and then they show unawareness, for example some one may say to another "You have grown big or you have grown so faster" and in response another say "Are you sure? /You are kidding! /You are lying/Tell me it's not true/Are you serious?" This is the time when people go in mirrors to observe themselves whether what others are saying is true. No one can stop him or her self from growing too slow or too fast therefore everyone has to observe and utilize time, knowing that every time that passes in a day its purpose is to add another year to the years he/she has (when growth also is taking time). The movement of time is very fast that's why babies who had days, weeks, months, or one year are now people with 20, 30, 50 or 100 years.

CHAPTER TEN

OBSERVING TIME

If people could observe time then they would have used all days well. People should teach themselves how to observe time. People should put on watches and have clocks at home and in offices that whenever they look at them they remember that time is running off and there is a need to observe and use it effectively. Many people without watches or clocks pass a lot of time. These people keep on asking others the time - that is, "what is the time?"…after they are told the time, they show unawareness and imagine how the time has gone. They keep on saying "I was to do this and that before this time", so they start to panic in the last hours.

The early clocks were good at making people observe time. They had bells that rang at every hour. This made people to observe the movement of time at every ring of the clock bell hence utilizing the time well and effectively. Today alarm clock and cellular phone with alarm have helped people to observe and utilize time. These alarms have made people to wakeup very early for prayers, planning business, plan for the future, and many others. A big number of people, who are very early at work every day, use these alarm clocks and cellular phones alarm to wakeup very early.

Most of the people focus on the today's year and they do not look at the years in the future. This has taken place by the current calendars. There is no calendar for years only. A normal calendar includes days, weeks, months, and a year. It is very difficult to find a person with calendars or a calendar of 2013 to 2037. Therefore, this makes some people to focus on the year of the calendar they are in (today's year). Every thing they do and plan, they base on the calendar of today's year. People mark date(s) on calendar for doing things, for example meetings, business deals, or anything else. But if people had calendars of years to come they would have marked date(s) (on these calendars) of doing things in future and this would have made them to start now working for that date or day they have marked on that calendar of that year in future for example 2018, 2025, 0r 2039.

People look at calendars to know the date, days, weeks, and months but it is very difficult to find a person looking at a calendar to know (what is) the year we are in. For this matter, years tend to runoff when a person is not aware/noticing them. Because people have no calendars of the years to come, they only notice the run out of years at the end of the year. They always make statement like "this year has gone, we have entered another year"; "years are running very fast". Therefore, after this period, people do not make these statements anymore until another end of the year, and then they make these statements again. They do not make these statements in the middle of the year. They do not even say "this year have passed; let me utilize the coming year in a useful way".

Wise is a person when he/she start moving his/her life on time table(s). If you use a timetable, you will either utilize or waste your time willingly when you are aware. The timetable makes you to observe and utilize your time in a principled way. The timetable makes you to do your activities, work, businesses, and other works in specified time. The timetable becomes a commander of your thoughts and minds. It gives the minds what to do, instead of being idle lucking what to do. It also keeps you alert to observe and utilize your time well. Therefore, you should have a timetable and alarm clock to observe time well. It is very bad to remember something you had to do (earlier) when it is already late. Observing and utilizing time is not something to make in a right place, at a right time. Observing and utilizing time is for everywhere and at all time. If you have little time to observe and utilize time you will gain few things but if you have/put much time, you will gain much.

Do not worry about the time left, just use the time you have right now. If you enter an examination when it has started 30 minutes, do not look at the time past or the time left but focus on the time you have now. If you do this, you can get 50% instead of '10% if you looked at the time left and start to worry or panic'. In observing and utilizing time, we have to be firm and strong. Never panic doing something in the last hours. People have lost: dignity, self control, and even died because of trying to do a huge or big work/activity in a very small period. No one can fill a small cup/glass with a jerrycan of water. If a person make this then the cup will become full with water and pour out. It is better to move on timetable and following it in order to give yourself enough time of doing certain things, or else you will find it very difficult to change or do certain things when you are aged. It is better to start your journey of success now. Its good to do what you love most, what you think can lead you to your success and destination. No one wants to end up in bad situation/poverty. It is like in racing, those who run start at the same time/line but no one want to reach in the same time with anyone else. Everyone is fighting to make his/her end better and successful. Today every one is racing to finish up successful in life. If you do not use the time you have, you will be the last. Make sure no one is ahead of you in matters of observing and utilizing time, that you may be the first/great one among the successful people in the future. If you lose/waste anytime, someone else will take your number/position. Remember, in racing there is a time that reaches especially at the last lap when no one can run more (ahead) than another but just moving in the same distance according to his or her position. This last lap is like moving wheels of a vehicle, the behind tyres cannot move faster that the front tyres. Therefore, keep your position by observing and utilizing every time you have/get. If you waste any time, your opportunities will go else where to another person who will add those opportunities to his/her self then his/her position will move up from his/her current position. Everyone has his/her own opportunities. Your opportunities are not for anyone else. However, if you waste time you also waste opportunities. These wasted opportunities will go to other people. Time is limited and waits for no man. If you play around with time, you are destroying your future because time always ignores everything. It moves the same as usually. If you start giving out reasons of not observing and utilizing time, you will fail. However-much your reasons are strong, time will ignore your reasons and will stay moving as usual.

Time is what brings and what removes. No one should be deceived that his/her beauty will remain forever. It is time that will make that person a very old woman/man and he/she will see no beauty again. You may not like this but it is the truth, people who hate to be told the truth about them, everyone always deceives them. If am to ask, "Did you want to stay a young child feeding on milk forever?" You do not regret your growth from childhood to teenage/youth/adult/man/woman/aged. Therefore, if you liked that change then you will not run away from the changes that are to happen in the future. What am trying to say to you is that, your look does not matter but what you are is what matters. However much a child of a rich man/woman is ugly, to the society this child is handsome/beautiful. If you have wealthy then you are the most handsome/beautiful. Therefore, do not waste your time in luxury things. Have your time in making up a successful future. In some countries, rich people shine even more than their leaders. The rich people make decisions on the finance of the state/nation. The government takes these people's decisions important as those of leaders. Today use your time and it will make for you tremendous wealthy such that in future you can be one of those who have permission and power to decide on the state/country's budget and development plans. You have to know that with time, you can buy money and the money you get can buy much time again. On that job/work you are employed, you are selling your time to your employer in order to get money, then use that money to start up your business and you will get jobseekers who will like to sell their time to you by working in your business/company.

Time has been there since the creation of the world. It is still here even now. Generations have come and pass, people born and die, great thing come and go, but time is still in place even now. In every generation there will time because it is time that makeup a generation(s). Time beautifies and wears. It has made beautiful people old, rose flowers to dry, new clothes to old clothes, new fashion to old fashion. We can know what time will change/bring in the future. Therefore be on your alert, that if you waste time, it may bring in your way what you do not like/want. For example, the scholars who waste time in entertainment and funs instead of spending their time in reading books always fail exams. Moreover, a big number of them find life difficult after school. It is better to look in the future than to look only where you are. If you look only where you are then you are like some one who rest on the way before reaching his/her destiny. If you look on the little success you have now, it may be very difficult to focus on the success in future. What you sow is what you reap. If you use your time now, you will gain it in future; but if you spare it, you will have nothing in future. If you use your time then you are making it to be productive that in future it may deliver/produce much time. The choice is yours either to retire at an early age or to work the rest of your life. Failure to observe and utilize time is failure to prosper in life.

Never say "I will do this or that tomorrow" if you postpone things to do them tomorrow then there are few chance of doing them. Most of the people keep on saying "I will do this/that tomorrow". Then every day they will say, "I will do tomorrow", and their tomorrow will never end because everyday they will keep on saying the same. In addition, this becomes the same story repeatedly. Whatever you want to do - now is the time. If some one tells you to do something, look at the way and speed he/she uses then use that. Whatever you do, do it fast and now. The hour to do everything is now. Now is the time to start. If you are preparing something next week, then start now such that next week does not come when you have changed your mind or lost interest in doing it. Have you ever planned of doing something tomorrow and then tomorrow you postpone it to another day and another day. Therefore, its better you do now. Some people do not have patience when they need something that is why they get what they want very quick/fast. Not having patience has its advantages and disadvantages, but living all factors constant, in observing and utilizing time we need to be fast in certain things. If you want to buy clothes in the new stock, at a certain boutique, and you are willing to go tomorrow then you will find the nice clothes/dresses taken by people who will go today to the same boutique. You should be observing and utilizing time in today's activities, if you waste time today, you are wasting opportunities. If you keep on saying, "I will do this or that tomorrow" then you are to take what is not the best. Start to do something now to get the best in future. If you want to buy a land, a plot, or a house, then buy it today because tomorrow you may find it taken or if not taken, its price is going to increase/rise. There is no time to waste. In wasted time, it is where people waste opportunities. If you are to do anything today never postpone it to another day because it will become very expensive tomorrow.

The fear that people have in doing some things makes them to go on postponing activities to other days. If you do not stop that fear in you then you will waste a lot of time and opportunities. Therefore, other people will get the opportunities you have wasted and make them to turn into success. Success in life is to those who uses there time well, those who have ability to do things right now.

Observing and utilizing every time does not mean that you do not rest or do not have leisure. If your timetable is showing leisure, let it be leisure and if showing activities let it be activities. However, have much time in activities and less time in active leisure.

CHAPTER ELEVEN

PASSING TIME

Today is the yesterday of tomorrow. Tomorrow if you are to be glad in your yesterday, you have to work hard today. Today, tomorrow, and forever are days of doing great activities therefore make sure you utilize them well. It is not good to make statements like "I am passing time" or "we are passing time". Today you find many people who keep on saying "we are passing time". Every one should be away of all the passing of time and start now to do something. Remember, time is driving many people the way it want and they cannot say, "Stop" and it respond. They just leave time to take them wherever it wants. However, to control over time it is for only those who start today to work for their future. No one can make time to go backward and no one can make time to move faster or run forward.

Never waste any single second of an hour in a day or a night. It is very difficult to change what has past. In the few hours ago…think…what have you done in them? If you have utilized them its well but if you have wasted them, they are already gone, now you have to utilize the time you have right now. Entertainment makes time to run at a microsecond speed. When a person have fun/entertainment his or her thoughts and minds put all attention on it, and here time runs more quickly because he/she has nothing that will bother him/her to look at the watch/clock. People in entertainment want time to move slowly such that they may continue enjoying fun and entertainment. In entertainment, time will run very quickly yet you see as if time is moving/running slow, and at the end, you will spend the all day doing nothing productive. People make plans of going somewhere at specified time but because of fun and entertainment, they forget and later get to know that they had planned to go somewhere when the fun and entertainment is over. These people who are in funs and entertainment to them time looks to be not running because there is no way a person can observe time when his or her minds/thoughts are on entertainment. Then when the entertainment is over that is when a person starts to observe time, thinking of doing things which were to be done earlier. For example people after entertainment tend to say, "I was to do this and that", "I was to go this way and that way" but when is too late.

      Entertainment covers the time of doing some activities/work a person would have done. Then time and days move on without any productive work done. Too much entertainment makes day and night to come and pass when people have not utilized them well. People enter cinema halls when its day (morning or noon) and come out when it has come to night. Then they start to ask them selves "when did it come to night, I thought it was still day". When the thought or minds are entertained, the focus on the entertainment does not leave any space of observing and utilizing time. Take an example of people working in town and city malls, buildings, arcades, or plazas. They sit a lot and become bored in their shops. They usually see time as not running. Some make statement like "when will it come to evening and I go back home". This has led many to buy televisions (TVs), radio systems, computers, and others things to get entertainment such that they do not get bored - thus obstructing their minds/thoughts from observing the movement of time. In watching movies, computer games, music videos, and others things, makes a lot of time to pass unutilized. Unless when in entertainment/funs is where you earn. Most people move out of the arcades or malls not knowing that it has come to night. They use the watches, phones, and clocks to know the time. Today entertainment is everywhere in the world that is why today every person says, "These days/years are running faster than the days/years of long ago.

Many people in towns and cities walk and work with entertainment. For example, people work while listen to music using earphones connected to small radio receivers, PDA, or cellular phones. Therefore, these people instead of thinking about other things, their minds are on the music in their ears. This loud music in ears cannot make a person to think or plan something.

"An idle mind is a devil's workshop". People have replaced idleness with funs, entertainment, games, and many other things in order not to be idle. If you are idle, you are going to give way to many thoughts /minds. If you are not idle, your thoughts/minds are controlled but when you are idle, your minds have many thoughts that are either bad or good. However, when people are idle, the bad thoughts become stronger than the good ones. That is why idleness is a devil's workshop. When some people are idle, they develop many thoughts and fail to control them. So instead of being idle, use this time to plan for your future. Do not follow bad thoughts. If a person is idle today, then he/she should make a plan of not being idle again tomorrow. If a person decides to go for entertainment, then he will be idle again tomorrow. Therefore, you have to get a place free from all entertainment, and plan for your tomorrow. Take an example of people who plan for businesses, who read books, who writing novels, or those who research on certain things how they do; they look for places that are quiet with no sound or noise and come up with solutions. However, when in open places or entertainment they cannot do anything because all the attention is on moving pictures and sounds. Therefore, you should get time away from all kind of work/entertainment and use this time to plan/prepare your future and business. Makeup your mind today then tomorrow will be a better day for you, your family and the people around you. Do not be idle to give the devil space to tempt you.

Never allow any one to waste your time. You should be on your watch about your time. Many people are ready to waste your time but be firm and strong to refuse this to happen. Many people want others to give their time to them but for them do not give time to others. Never change your schedule or timetable to go on other people's plans, unless when you earn from them. Give your time where you earn or where you are helping others in need. People should not take time for granted. Time is what everyone is looking and fighting for. On this earth everything base on time. Those in prison who were imprisoned for crimes, some want time to run very fast while others want it to move very slowly. For example, those who are serving their sentence of 3 years imprisonment want time to run/move very fast whereas those who are under sentence of death want time to move very slow. Everyone wants time to move according to the condition/situation he/she is passing through. Most people forward one hour especially in summer and spring such that evenings have more daylight and mornings have less. However, time will not change/stop because someone is in a situation or a condition that needs time to forward or rewind. Time will stay moving as usual.

Wasted time leave gaps behind that are difficult to fill. It is rather better to observe and utilize the time you have now that it does not leave gaps again.

CHAPTER TWELVE

GOD CONTROLLING TIME

If you are out of time then you are remaining with only one choice. Moreover, that choice is to turn to the Lord God and Jesus Christ. Every person is fighting to live in time. If you separate from time then you are to die but if you remain in time, you are to live long. No one can add time to his/her time. No one can control time except one that is God. It is God who created day and night, who created the sun and the moon and commanded all their movements. In addition, there movement brings about time. In Joshua 10: 12-13…Then Joshua spoke to the Lord in the day when the Lord delivered up the Amorites before the children of Israel, and he said in the sight of Israel: "Sun, stand still over Gibeon; And Moon, in the Valley of Aijalon."………So the sun stood still, And the moon stopped, Till the people had revenge Upon their enemies…….Is this not written in the book of jasher? So the sun stood still in the midst of heaven, and did not hasten to go down for about a whole day. If your time is running out then only God can make it to stop in one place such that your time does not run out. In addition, the Lord God is the one who can add time on the time people have on the earth. This is in Isaiah 38:1….In those days Hezekiah was sick and near death. And Isaiah the prophet, the son of Amoz, went to him and said to him," Thus says the Lord: 'Set your house in order, for you shall die and not live.'"……then Hezekiah turned his face towards the wall, and prayed to the Lord……and said, "Remember now, O Lord, I pray, how I have walked before you in truth and with a loyal heart, and have done what is good in your sight. "And Hezekiah wept bitterly…And the word of the Lord came to Isaiah, saying…. "Go and tell Hezekiah, Thus says the Lord, the God of

David your Father: "I have heard your prayer, I have seen your tears; surely I will add to your days fifteen years. A year is a make up of time. It is a makeup of time to come up with a day, a week, a month, a year or years. The years a person has, is the time he/she has spend on earth. God decided the years (amount of time) which people have to live on the earth. Genesis 6:3....And the Lord said, "My Spirit shall not strive with man forever, for he is indeed flesh; yet his days shall be one hundred and twenty years." A person with years of age above 120 year shows God's mercy on him/her. God gives these extra years (time) to a person. Whoever wants to live more than 120 years should believe in the Lord God and Jesus Christ. Many people have given testimonies of life. Some people where to the point of death but God gave them more time and now they are living. If you want to live long then the only way to have long life is to believe in God and Jesus Christ. Believe in Jesus Christ who has authority in heaven and on earth. In Matthew 28:18, .And Jesus came and spoke to them, saying, all authority has been given to Me in heaven and on earth. Jesus Christ has authority to give you unlimited time on earth and everlasting life if you believe in Him.

Whenever you do charitable deeds, God gives you more time on earth. Helping the poor, food to the hungry, accommodation to the homeless, clothes to naked, Medicine/treatment to the sick; seeking justice, defending and pleading for the poor, the orphans, the widows, and the disabled. If you do these, then you get much time on earth. If you were to die then you will not die but you will live long on earth because of helping and supporting people in need. In Acts 9:39-40....Then Peter arose and went with them. When he had come, they brought him to the upper room. And all the widows stood by him weeping, showing the tunics and garments which Dorcas had made while she was with them…But Peter put them all out, and knelt down and prayed. And turning to the body he said, "Tabitha, arise." And she opened her eyes, and when she saw Peter she sat up.....Then he gave her his hand and lifted her up; and when he had called the saints and the widows, he presented her alive. For the Lord God and His son Jesus Christ created man. In Genesis 1:26 then God said, "Let Us make man in Our image, according to Our likeness; - God who created man and gave him life is also able to limit and to unlimited the life (time) of man. It was the sin that Adam and Eve made that made God to limit the time of man on earth through death. In Genesis 3:19…In the sweat of your face you shall eat bread…Till you return to the ground, For out of it you were taken; For dust you are, And to dust you shall return. Now Jesus Christ makes us to live in unlimited time. He died for us and His blood removes our sins that we got right from Adam and Eve. In 2Corinthians 5:17…Therefore, if anyone is in Christ, he is a new creation; old things have passed away; behold, all things have become new. Jesus Christ the son of God takes away all the curses (that were cursed man in the book of Genesis 3:15 to 19) from whoever believes in Him. All people can live in unlimited time on the earth if they believe in Jesus Christ the son of God.

If some one is running out of time, whom will he/she call to save him/her? Only our Lord Jesus Christ the son of God can save a person from death. In Romans 10:13...For "whoever calls on the name of the Lord shall be saved." If anyone is running out of time, let him/her call the name "Jesus Christ".

CONCLUSION

Most of the people when they read such statements above in this book their minds become 100% willing to do what they have read. In addition, there are completely set to what they have read about but when time pass by, they forget or lose willingness of doing what they have read. This means that the complete desire to do that very thing they have read about is there at the time they are reading. However, in just hours, days, or weeks; what someone has read about is no longer in his or her minds and it is no longer new but old. You have to try to avoid this by putting something to make you remember what you have read. You should also put this book on your daily timetable. To a person, observing and doing what he or she has read about is not easy at all.

Become a doer of what you have read about but not reading only. Anything you read about becomes useful when you put it in action. If you do not practice what you read then you are reading for nothing. For example, on 100% only 80% of people read and do not observe/do, 15% read and become willing to do what they have read, but after they do not. In addition, 5% only read and practice what they have read about which turns into success but then after some time almost a year, 3% persist on doing what they read about and it become part of them, which makes them billionaires, and successful forever.

What you practice every day soon will become part of you. Always put in action what you read. The time is now therefore start working out what you have read. Remember past is past and will never come back neither will it be found any where except reading/remembering it in history.

www.ingramcontent.com/pod-product-compliance
Lightning Source LLC
Chambersburg PA
CBHW050810180526
45159CB00004B/1610